ROLF HEIMANN'S
PUZZLE MAZIA

Perplexing puzzles & maddening mazes

LITTLE HARE

Little Hare Books
4/21 Mary Street, Surry Hills
NSW 2010 AUSTRALIA

www.littleharebooks.com

Copyright © Rolf Heimann 2004

First published in 2004
Reprinted in 2005

National Library of Australia
Cataloguing-in-Publication entry

Heimann, Rolf, 1940-.
Puzzlemazia.

For children
ISBN 1 877003 64 6.

1. Maze puzzles – Juvenile literature. 2. Puzzles –
Juvenile literature. I. Title.

793.73

Designed by ANTART
Produced by Phoenix Offset, Hong Kong
Printed in China

5 4 3 2

Beetle reunion

Will these two beetles be able to meet? With your help they will!

Temple teaser

Find your way through the maze to the temple.

Escape from the castle
Can you escape from the castle's turret?

Wrong window

There are 20 windows in the castle, all the same—except one. Can you spot which one?

Faulty flag

One of the flags is wrong, too!

Tricky squares

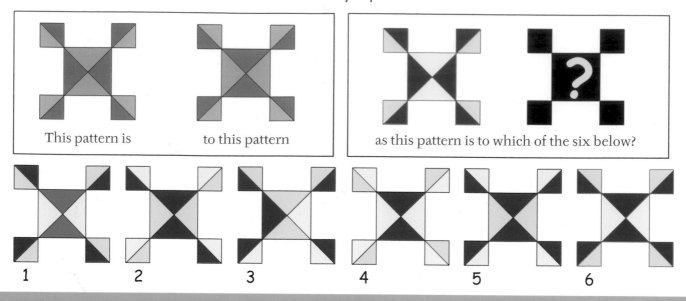

This pattern is   to this pattern   as this pattern is to which of the six below?

1   2   3   4   5   6

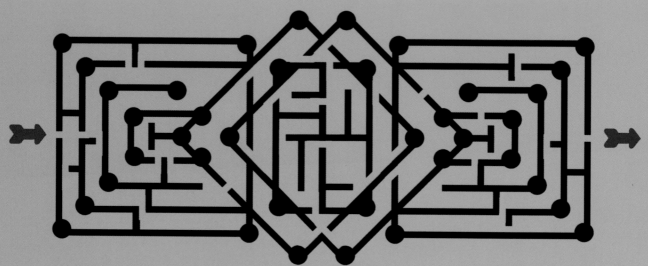

Easy come, easy go
This might look like an easy maze—but don't be deceived!

Diamonds are forever
But don't take forever to find which gem fits the blank space below!

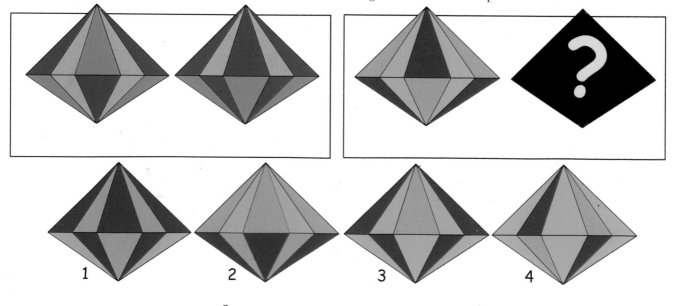

1   2   3   4

Lucky bug

Only one of these bugs can reach the flower.
Which one?

Ship ahoy!

If you want to get into the lifeboat that belongs to this ship, you'd better look closely—
which one of the boats in the water should you choose?

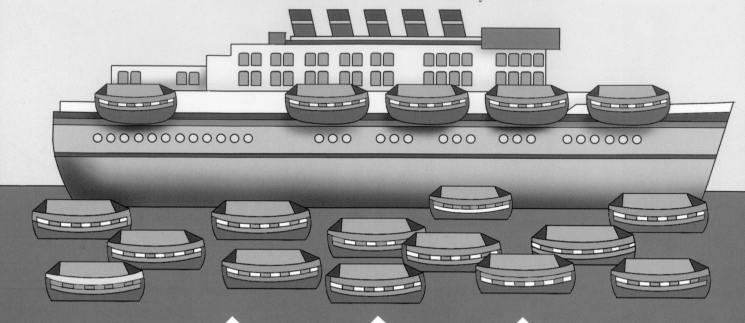

Trapped

Help the yellow fish
out of the maze and
into the open sea!

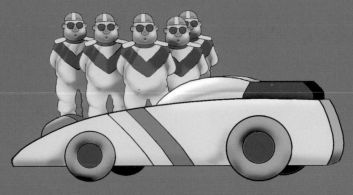

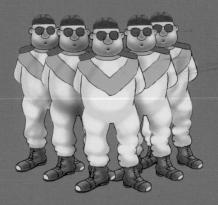

Pit stop problem

The uniforms of the pit stop crew match the cars they service.
Which of the six cars below is the one for the waiting team?

1

2

3

4

5

6

Be quick!

If you can do this maze in 30 seconds flat, you'll be a hit with the pit stop crew!

Lend a hand!
The whole maze has to be
painted blue, so grab a brush
and find your way to the last
bit of yellow.

Two of a kind
Though their sizes may differ, two of the fish in the school above resemble each other exactly.

What colour is the ball in my hand?

An educated guess
After studying the number of balls on the table, can you guess the colour of the ball in the man's hand?

Sail away

What numbers should go on the pink hull, and on the reefed sail of the last ship?

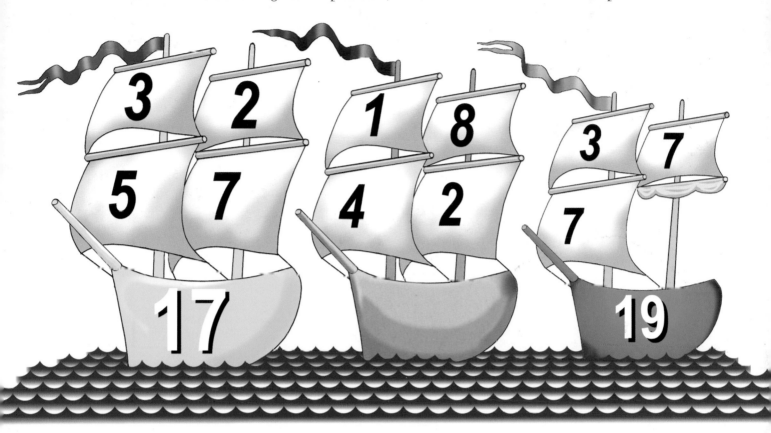

Paper flotilla

Only one of these paper boats was made of the paper on which the flotilla sits.

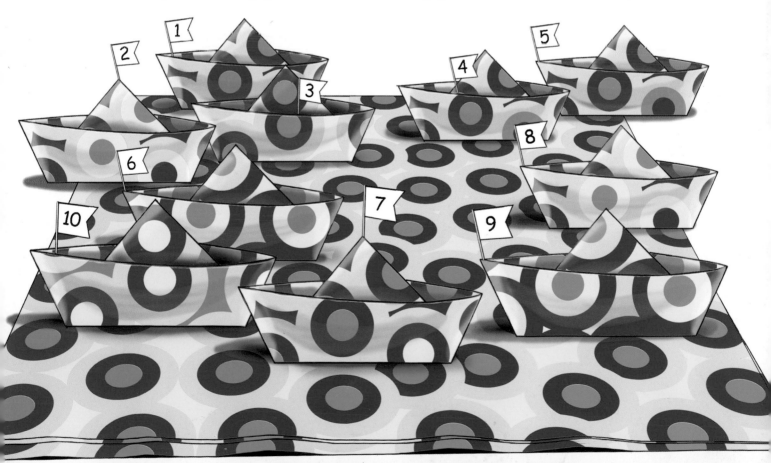

Day 1 Day 2 Day 3 Day 4 Day 5

Day 6 ? Day 7 Day 8 Day 9 Day 10

Changing flowers

The floral arrangement is changed according to a regular system—
every day a new flower is added, but each flower only lasts three days before it is removed.
What would the arrangement look like on Day 7?

1 2 3 4 5 6

Wheels within wheels
You might get dizzy going through this maze, but don't give up!

Upstairs, downstairs

It's a long way from the lake to the flower garden—especially with all those stairs to climb!

Wall art

An artist has taken a lot of care to paint the correct emblem of the Gardeners' Guild on the walls. He only made one mistake...Can you spot it?

Lure of the lily

Love lilies are a delicacy for red-backed beetles.
Which one of these four will reach the prize?

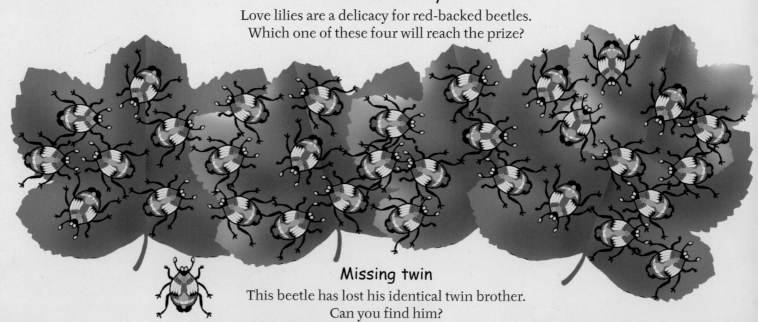

Missing twin

This beetle has lost his identical twin brother.
Can you find him?

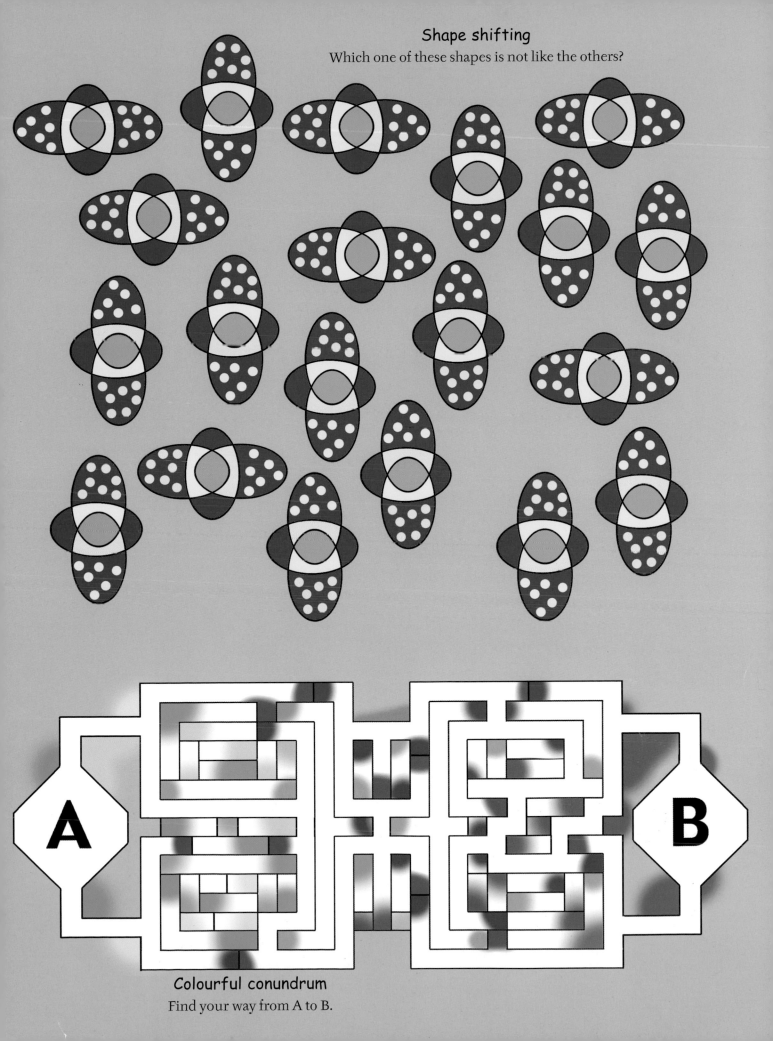

Shape shifting
Which one of these shapes is not like the others?

Colourful conundrum
Find your way from A to B.

Wiggly worries

These three children are looking for their pet snake, Rover. Can you help them?

He has red eyes

...and a red tail

...and red spots all over.

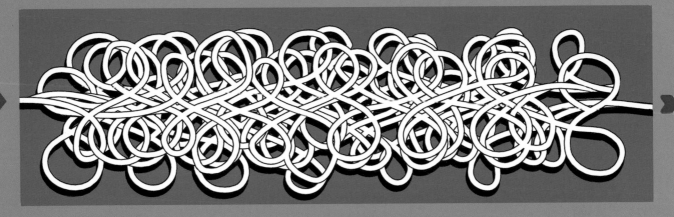

Tangled twine
Don't cross any black lines!

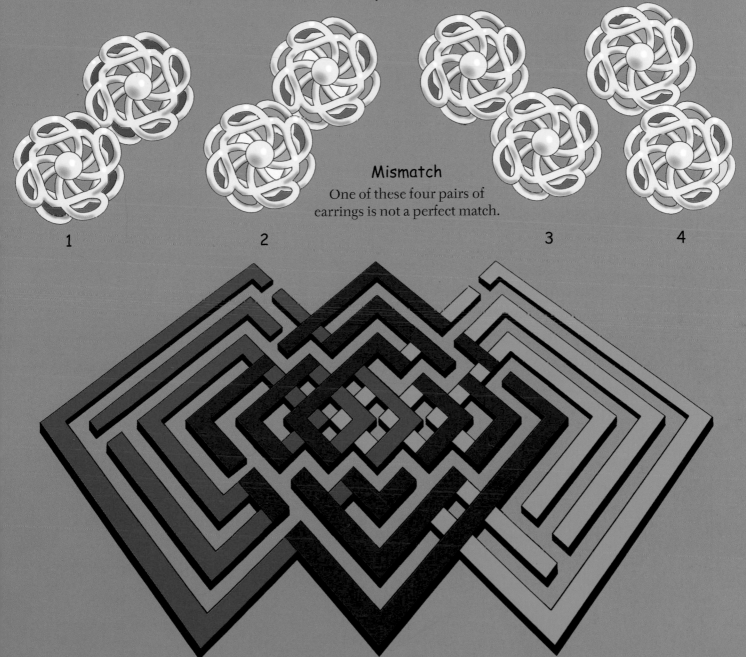

Mismatch
One of these four pairs of
earrings is not a perfect match.

1   2   3   4

Easy breezy
Try this maze—it's a breeze!

Gone fishing

Some people will go to any length to find a good fishing spot! Help this fisherman through the maze to the fishpond.

Snake tails

How many snakes are on this page? Sometimes the tails are all you can see!

Mystery shards

Which of the ten shapes below fits the
blank space in the figure to the right?
(Rotate the shape if necessary!)

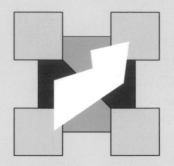

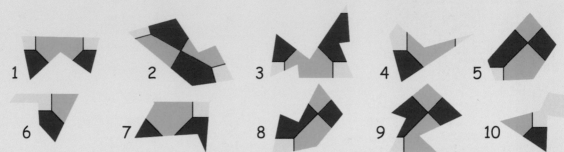

1

2

3

4

5

6

7

8

9

10

Dodge the confetti

Keep to the white lines!

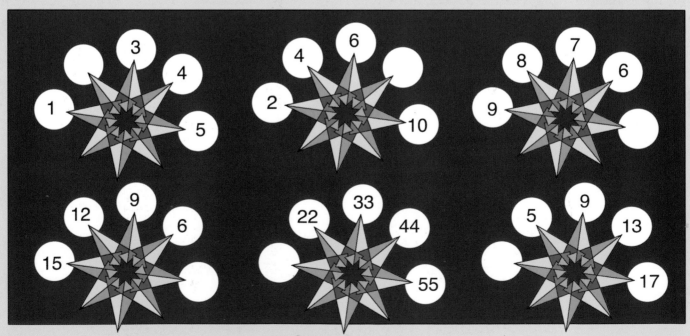

Star system

Filling in the blanks is easy—just follow the system!

Target practice

Each of the four competitors in the archery competition has their own kind of arrow. Who won?

The shivering seven

Nothing, not even freezing temperatures, will stop the seven gentlemen of the Polar Bear Club from having their weekly swim—except if they forget their towels! Which of the Polar Bears has forgotten his towel today?

Pieces of eight

Now try to find the eight shapes below hidden in the picture!

Solutions

Beetle reunion

Brothers in arms
As Tiger is to his brother
Regit

Temple teaser

Escape from the castle
Wrong window
Faulty flag

Tricky squares
Number 6

Easy come, easy go

Diamonds are forever
Number 2

Lucky bug

Ship ahoy
Trapped

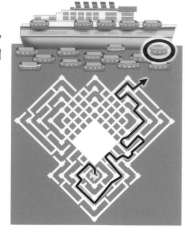

Pit stop problem
Number 4

Be quick!

Lend a hand!

Two of a kind

An educated guess
A pink ball. There
are 10 balls of every
other colour, but
only nine pink balls.

Sail away
The numbers on the sails
add up to the number on
the hull.

Paper flotilla
Number 3

Changing flowers
Number 4

Wheels within wheels

Upstairs downstairs

Wall art

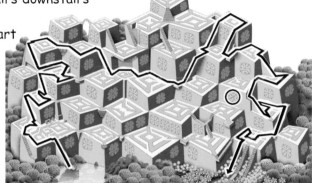

Lure of the lily

Missing twin

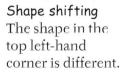

Shape shifting
The shape in the top left-hand corner is different.

Colourful conundrum

Wiggly worries

Tangled twine

Mismatch
Number 4

Gone fishing
Snake tails

Mystery shards
Number 2

Dodge the confetti

Star system

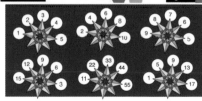

Target practice
Tina has 11 points, Liz has 10, Bob has 9 and Ted has 5.

The shivering seven
Pieces of eight

Rolf Heimann was born in Dresden, Germany in 1940. In 1945, he witnessed the total destruction of his home city—which made him a lifelong opponent of war.

At age 18 he migrated to Australia. Over the next few years he worked his way around the country doing all kinds of jobs, including fruit-picking, labouring at railways and working in factories. Every spare hour was spent writing and sketching. Eventually, he settled in Melbourne, where he worked for printers and publishers before finally running his own art studio.

In 1974, Rolf sailed his own boat around the Pacific (and met his future wife, Lila, in Samoa), returning to Australia after two years to concentrate on painting, writing, cartooning and illustrating. He has now published over twenty books of puzzles and mazes, several junior novels and a picture book. His books have travelled to dozens of countries, and have sold millions of copies around the world.

Also by Rolf Heimann from Little Hare Books:
CRAZY COSMOS
BRAIN BUSTING BONANZA
ASTROMAZE
ZOODIAC

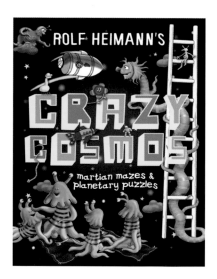

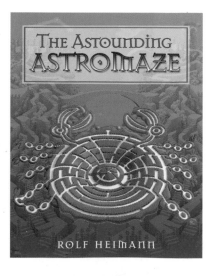